DIRT EATERS

PREVIOUS SNOWBOUND CHAPBOOK
AWARD WINNERS

Barbara Tran, *In the Mynah Bird's Own Words,* selected by Robert Wrigley

David Hernandez, *A House Waiting for Music,* selected by Ray Gonzalez

Mark Yakich, *The Making of Collateral Beauty,* selected by Mary Ruefle

Joy Katz, *The Garden Room,* selected by Lisa Russ Spaar

Cecilia Woloch, *Narcissus,* selected by Marie Howe

John Cross, *staring at the animal,* selected by Gillian Conoley

Stacey Waite, *the lake has no saint,* selected by Dana Levin

Brandon Som, *Babel's Moon,* selected by Aimee Nezhukumatathil

Kathleen Jesme, *Meridian,* selected by Patricia Fargnoli

Anna George Meek, *Engraved,* selected by Ellen Doré Watson

Deborah Flanagan, *Or, Gone,* selected by Christopher Buckley

Chad Parmenter, *Weston's Unsent Letters to Modotti,* selected by Kathleen Jesme

Allan Peterson, *Other Than They Seem,* selected by Ruth Ellen Kocher

Matt Donovan, *Rapture & the Big Bam,* selected by Lia Purpura

Eliza Rotterman   # DIRT EATERS

T|P

TUPELO PRESS
North Adams, Massachusetts

Dirt Eaters.
Copyright © 2018 Eliza Rotterman. All rights reserved.

Library of Congress Catalog-in-Publication data available upon request.
ISBN: 978-1-946482-05-1

Cover and text designed and composed in Adobe Garamond and Chong Old Style by Ann Aspell.
Cover art: Amanda Acker, "Grass Shadow" (2015). Gouache on paper, 12 x 12 inches. Used with permission of the artist (www.pinterest.com/source/aacker.bigcartel.com/).

First edition: June 2018.

Other than brief excerpts for reviews and commentaries, no part of this book may be reproduced by any means without permission of the publisher. Please address requests for reprint permission or for course-adoption discounts to:
Tupelo Press
P.O. Box 1767, North Adams, Massachusetts 01247
(413) 664–9611 / editor@tupelopress.org / www.tupelopress.org

Tupelo Press is an award-winning independent literary press that publishes fine fiction, nonfiction, and poetry in books that are a joy to hold as well as read. Tupelo Press is a registered 501(c)(3) nonprofit organization, and we rely on public support to carry out our mission of publishing extraordinary work that may be outside the realm of the large commercial publishers. Financial donations are welcome and are tax deductible.

to my mother

CONTENTS

DIRT EATERS

The multiplying wood

I call this pageantry, your green
evering towards blue, an intelligent
loneliness. I feel supernatural,
consider one day a child
may ease down from the sky.
We'll collect moss and lichen,
adapt to the bitterness of roots.

There is a shoreline trail,
a rankled lake. I throw rocks
to please her, devise a plan
for a raft. Mother and child
paddling out, a blue forest chorusing,
and in a quiet, non-nuclear way,
the sun enters the last era of light.

Light-rope

In my own made-up dark
I understand light as ash falling from god falling from injury.
The light-rope dangling and a mother's
adolescence is a gun
left in the body. A bright liquid night
spit on the sheets and drying
like the pulp of an apricot. The sun
today is hysterical or maybe I'm in love
in another life. I'm looking at you
looking at the sea. I'm shouting at the waves.
Anything, you lied, can happen.

Light-rope

Goodbye, I shudder.
A scientist, so I study wading birds, bones of the wrist,
love in retrospect. Variation
is light recombinant, peregrine. Evolution
is not what anyone would choose, nor the orderly
inheritance of traits. Rather a neutron star,
the crush of twenty times twenty into one,
centers dense with rupture. *Love,*
stay close to the wreckage,
my orange life-vest, a flower.

It wasn't our fault; it was a light-cluster

Wandering ice-moon, your voice is smoky,
a forest from childhood

I lived in Ohio, nothing burned
except adolescence, a radio
in a neighbor's basement

Like the others we gazed at stars,
the galaxy of pain with its red dwarves
crossing the galaxy of pleasure,

a single fold of brilliance

Murrain

It was time to get up and go.
Time to wake and dredge — lipstick, ring tones,
mineral debris. It was time to pile up,
and we were all together, holding snow.
Heads confused with nylons, sponges, spatulas, pillows.
We leaked digital residue,
found paring knives, bricks.
We watched a talk show and another
on forensic discoveries.
                              We were hungry.
Found a recipe for caramel-nut brownies.
In the cupboards, mountains of quartz.
Granite, basalt scars.
Someone said, my body is in a warming period,
so we assumed the anatomical position,
conjured the melting sensation.
Inside, the body's wet silk,
plastic — a wind-up piggy, a yellow pail.
Instructions for planting a garden.
We wanted to wield tools with authority.
We wanted our mothers to hand us something soft
and new: a kitten in a striped sock,
a shoebox containing nature: acorns, leaves,
a baby squirrel to bottle-feed.
                              Instead
we made crushing sounds. We wrote
the doctor's words and stared at our hands.

The right lung fills with fluid.
Kidneys dry up.
                    They worked to remove
the sick tree in sections, the broadleaf maple,
that since October, had begun to lean.
It may have fallen into the living room.
It may have pinned the dog to her chair.
We said goodbye.
There was a great show of weeping, digging.
A show of objects heaped.
The glacier slid and churned.
Homes and grief, days and sheets.
The glacier retreated.
Strands of collagen, rudiments, rock.
This, my pelvic talus,
this, my ovum, my inland sea.
We tried once more to understand
what tomorrow would be like.
A trillion buckling knees.
Salt and lathes.
                    Summers unswum.
The radio played a song. I turned it off,
wrote, *It's time* on the wall in butter.
Time to disassemble.

                    I cleared a space

I stood in the field, held up my arms

I keep growing towards the providence of angels,
                              wakeful, ataxic
Agitation, an orange crow, a rake
scratching, were their songs like saws
                    or saws like songs?

And what is recovery
if not depletion, a sweetness
withheld, the smallest box in the body
                              opening

                        Inevitable,
            the arrival of flowers, it's spring
            after all, it's a goddamn orchard
            throttling the air with rupture

Are you not a part of this?
The way they walked up to us,
saying nothing

The feeling of a dress
                  lifting

Dirt eaters

I asked the law if it knew anything
about gravity, osmosis,
women walking home at night.
The law was quiet as a pumpkin
then offered to buy me a drink.
When I woke, the light was orange.

Populist and free of irony,
trees employ special chemical processes,
transduce light into sugar, sugar into time.
Women labor to maintain
an aboveground appearance,
fresh and unstressed.

It's troubling what you might call
transcendence.
Or, it's winter.
Survival, a red bell
behind the sun.

The home in America
is the most dangerous place
for women. Pregnancy
when we are most likely to be kicked,
slapped, pushed.

We grow towards it,
this out-of-body light.
The body of your mother
a frequency, a wavelength.
Her mind
glinting like a spoon in a drawer
in a wall made of wood.

A woman can't help but aberrate.
Just look what she does
in that metamorphic bedrock.
She's practically naked.
Lactating
in the office
at eleven and again at two.

I overhear two women remark
on the slaughter of horses.
But they're still good, one exclaimed.
Then, *Like sorry,*
thanks for all the work you've done.
You're no longer needed.

I turn diagrammatic, margins, months.
A splayed anatomy book.
A pair of persimmons on the counter
is melancholic, depending on the hour.
It's 3 A.M.
Everyone is sleeping.

The town where the law grew up
wasn't anywhere special,
and the story, nothing beyond
the usual trajectory
of acquiring power through
incremental acts of self-deception.

I make a bed
beneath the table, remember
a pair of shoes, their complementary field.
Clicking rudiments,
fawns pulled from the highway.
Conclusions to suck.

The law spoke
as if the voice of reason
had found no truer outlet.
The law wore khaki and light blue.
How old are you?
How old were you
the first time a man touched you?

A woman complains,
I wish I could pull *that* off.
A sensational dress that didn't fit
the occasion. She was seventeen,
twenty-one, thirty-four, fifty-nine.
She was walking alone
every night in America.

Bands of dark light waver.
I walk in the middle of the street,
singing for the same reason
a dog raises the fur on her neck.

I am made of trenchant gold.
Uncertainty ripening
this winter into one million
ways to suffer and its opposite.

Follow me. From memory
we can lick our way back.

Another deer poem

Waves by and for the waves
A democracy is blue or blue-green, opalescent depending
I was held & given a fawn
We are holding fawns, fawn-spots eleven, twenty-five or seventeen depending
Hands were beautiful are beautiful will not let go
This wave is the tallest followed by the next tallest wave
Do you?   Yes, I have a child   Do you?   Yes, a boy
I am given another fawn, another fawn
Through all this the sun, bright as a round of fat
Round of metal birds firing into the muscle below the bright fat
Through all this wave after wave after wave of fawn-spots

I awoke in the modern sense

The clock quipped, morning ripened,
I clicked the image of late summer
falling to bruise and rot

I thought, *a circle is the shape of light obsessing its object*
But I stepped in, forgot
traffic changes state: solids turn liquid, colloidal

Inscrutable oily dots, we resist
what we know to be true
What else to do but drift –

O mind, you read the map the body composes as sadness,
axis around which hands pine

Hue to hue, today we walk like lovers,
orbiteers of a question unzipped

What else to do
but dance loss to the quick

The first refuses to sing, so sings

In a hutch I spooned rabbit stew,
       wrote a letter on the tame one's ear,
the wild one I left for the fox,
       the mute appetite of snow.
I sketched meadows stacked
       like sedimentary rock, regions of the brain,
horses bitten to run intractably back
       to fire. I knew by scent your body's
sly marauding. Peeled fruit wetting the palm,
       mineral taste on the tongue. I was young,
impetuous. I touched it twice
       and twice it bit to keep me nestled close.

Two girls

Our love was an iron bell,
unnerved by the train's brazen call,
meat and bones meat and bones.

We spoke like scissor blades,
confetti clicking the fan.

I would have stolen two horses
for us to ride up that ridge,

where we might sing,
pick their hooves clean.

We were tin moths
moving over brick towards the light.
Meat and bones meat and bones.

Dogs sleep in your palms

I want to slide a finger
in the tan one's mouth,
tell you I followed tracks

into the long night.
They left small piles of shit
beside bones glittering with frost.

I remind you what we already know.
The dogs, hard at some other work,
do not wake.

I wait for light to return a self I recognize

Desire spoons a hole and through it
I push the red doorbell, its contemplation
ringing down the green
walk of my body, my mouth
marrowing seeds

I watch you and know myself
in the slow parallel time
of another

A love-idea, I am a conduit for light
seeking blood seeking light
gone through

Andromeda left a floral smudge on the sky's glass

I was at work when a woman told me she wanted
to be put to sleep and sorrow closed its blue gardens around me.
I was wearing only one red glove at the bus stop,
noticing the crows high in the dusking of city trees,
a motherless drizzle holding my slung,
moon-seed face. Spooky neighboring galaxy,
is it true? How many dark-years
stand compressing in the velocity
of light ones? A whale is reduced to oil
as your breath flares in my ear,
carrying the yellow leaves
of my name.
It's three in the morning,
and light-headed as an embryo,
I'm falling towards my own
untraceable light.

Elegy

In every cell there is a gene that codes for its own destruction.
Codes, in this case, refers to a process
that neatly packages the cell and tags it.
Other cells, designed to clean up the body,
recognize this cell to be in a state of mess.
To clean up, in this case, means to eat.
A macrophage is a big eater.
At any given time, I am host to a mess and a big eater.
I didn't always write poems like this.
There was even a time when passion
staged queenly tsunamis.
I once tattooed blue on the inside of my left wrist,
while you tattooed joy on your chest.
Everything about you—the desert,
your home full of dust and broken things—
bones, lace and Star Trek in the afternoon—
was passing through a state of blue.
And so was I, since a state of blue occurs when two women
remain close yet, nonetheless, accept
a certain amount of distance.
Arizona is a state I have not visited since you moved
to Massachusetts. I've seen pictures
of your new life on the sea and lakes in New York.
I've thought of writing you a long letter

in which I tell you everything. This, along with
the simple, self-assigned task
of writing one statement about how I feel
each day has remained incomplete.
Autumn, on another note, has succeeded
in its herald of winter. The red leaves
on the blueberry diffuse light into a low, pink tone.
I felt sad when I had to leave.
I must be passing through a state of survival.
The coywolf has survived by discarding parts of coyote and wolf.
I have a friend who bought a house the neighbors
for years had been filling with trash.
She left only one thing: a nest
in the back of a drawer.
Finely shredded porn woven into a circle,
the impression of a body resting.

Acupuncture

In the pale inner calm of my forearms
     needles resonate, two poles
          from which densities and motives

bluely elaborate. I am in the city
     but above it, looking out from the second floor.
          It's raining so I close my eyes.

A silver argument
     extends to where sea and sky
          are yet to complete

dissolution. I was there
     yesterday in a thrift-store wetsuit,
          re-inhabiting the experience of immersion.

The part of me I can't see
     increases with depth. I call this my shadow body,
          the life navigating below. Brushing my legs,

a flick of vertebrae, the silk
     grip of kelp, a swarm of micro-currents
          dissipating. The last time I swam

it was a different ocean,
        a different expectation towards which
                I drifted.

My mind archives my body in time.
        This is a feeling, the rippling place, the foam
                where a cormorant just dove.

I can't tell you if my fears
        are becoming more numerous
                or more specific. The pericardium

is a double-membrane
        surrounding the heart.
                Layers slide against each other,

correspond to the points on my forearms
        where needles press.
                Last night the green waves:

an electrocardiogram
        traversed the screen.
                It's my job to interpret slope

and deflection, but wading out
        to where my feet can't touch I want
                the heart's unknowability, its physics

and failures to seep
        into another mind, another voyage.
                Last month and farther north a blue whale

washed up. I was one of four and as we
        approached, I felt as if I were unpacking
                gauze from a wound, the scar

a long way off.
        We took pictures:
                the exposed vertebrae,

the petal-like fins draped
        and white with a pattern of blue overlapping
                rings. The sun flared in the interstice of cloud and water.

No one could explain why the whale appeared
        to be boneless, like a broad shallow stone.
                I told my friend

I was going to think about the whale
        as I fell asleep, its large heart
                traveling districts of cold salt.

We closed in,
        pulled scarves over our noses,
                the death-musk a molecular shape

the oldest region of the brain
        recognizes. Maybe she was next to me
                or maybe she had turned

to walk back. It's not desire
        between us but something else. A frequency
                low and slow

like the color red, our thoughts
        sliding against each other
                in correspondence, elaborations, waves.

ACKNOWLEDGMENTS

Grateful acknowledgment is made to the editors of *Colorado Review, The Journal, The Laurel Review, The Los Angeles Review, Phoebe, Poetry Northwest, Quarterly West, TYPO,* and *The Volta,* in which versions of these poems first appeared, and to Squaw Valley Community of Writers and the Vermont Studio Center for their generous support. Deepest thanks to Tupelo Press, and to Jim Schley, a most patient and insightful editor. And to Stephen Massimilla, Sara Sutter, Emily Kendal Frey, Chloe Garcia Roberts, Consuelo Wise, Vanessa Norton, Kristin Allen, Elizabeth Anable, John Cash, Amanda Acker, Lauren Kinney, Cassie Johnson, and David Citino, thank you for reading drafts of these poems and inspiring me with your own fabulous work. And to my family and my partner Taylor, endless appreciation and love.

OTHER BOOKS FROM TUPELO PRESS

See our complete list at www.tupelopress.org